# The Dilemma of Writing a Poem

# The Dilemma of Writing a Poem

## Juan Garrido-Salgado

PUNCHER & WATTMANN

First published in 2023
Published by Puncher & Wattmann
PO Box 279
Waratah NSW 2298

info@puncherandwattmann.com

NATIONAL
LIBRARY
OF AUSTRALIA

A catologue record for this book is available from The National Library of Australia.

ISBN    9781922571724

Cover design by Miranda Douglas

Printed by Lightning Source International

# Contents

## On Poetica

## New political poems

# Mother Earth Poems

# On Poetica

You shall create beauty not to excite the senses
but to give sustenance to the soul.
— Gabriela Mistral

# The dilemma of writing a few verses

The dilemma of writing a poem without light,
without the amenities of paper and ink,
without the digital keyboard
But with memory correcting each verse
like a clock tired of telling the time,
a fallen rhythm into language
in the calm of the dawn.
Only then, re-reading it
from the blue caressing,
the dew on the glass in my window.
Only printing it in the flight
of the last waking dream.

# Look back to where the wound is

*(Volver la mirada donde está la herida)*

Look back to where the wound is
and let the day clean it, let the night lick it
with shadows that come to surround you with calm or pain.
The open wound arrives like a clock from the past,
anchored in your bleeding skin between the bones
of what you were yesterday—tangled up today.
The dry word on numb lips.
Breathing is a cascade of howls falling
through the blood, through the open sides of the skin.
"*When a star sinks into a black hole*". Ernesto Cardenal read
this verse to me before I left his Managua.

# Life is a table set up for us to live the day

1
I wait for the call of your green leaves,
Lorca's rushed canto
of that fruit which will come
floating, in the mystery of water,
in the depth of roots
who kiss the light of day,
on the lips of the father sun.

We are fruit of those warm aromas
that feed our souls
and make us love the simple mystery
of each verse growing, in the broccoli
from the garden where I live.

2
A dry leaf falls in the verse.
The ink moans in its texture,
giving the winter a melody.
The rain tunes its violins.
The verse gives me a silhouette,
rolling like a tear on the window.

Which is the country, which is the true?
— Judith Wright

**1**
Country and the true are often irreconcilable.
There are like two banks from a long river,
where fish and water were poison bubbles left by the colonizers
killing the air of the earth,
killing the people of the land.
30 years ago, I didn't know Country well
but the truth was to my conscience like daily bread.
They buried it with bones and blood like an act of terror,
in the land where I come from, following the other poet: Gabriela
Mistral.

**2**
¿Cuál es este país?
Australia, the country that I live in now—
Always was, always will be Aboriginal Land.
It is the truth that Judith Wright gifts to us,
We citizens living on stolen land,
The Terra Nullius of Captain Cook,
still in 2021 is an unanswered question
What is this country?
It is a question born within the poet's conscience.
After a time of conflict, where war was the language
that the poet refuses to speak.
After thirty years of living in this land,
I can answer her question in this poem Spring after War.

3

the country
must be
a place
where
respect for all beings
be the morning sun
where the stories
be counted by those who suffered
evil
and at dusk
the air you breathe
gives us brotherhood
and when night comes
make us enjoy the peace
until happiness
to know that the truth
will wake up from our sunken rib
in the land of our ancestors.

4

Which is the truth?
This country has
more than 60 thousand years
before the colonist shootings,
poisoning and starving the first inhabitants,
now is the time for us to say: Makarrata
The truth is to say sorry

for what still happens to the stolen generations and for deaths in
custody.
Which is the truth?  Ask the poet.
It is a verse of dust on a white page
where words spring like a canto from the heart of the earth.

**5**

The land flourishes.

Fire burns the forests.

Blood buries the bones.

The fruits are wings in the wind.

Under the ashes grows the silence of war.

I embrace a poem in another language,
a poem from a resistance land.
A voice welcomes us into this country
that was born long before.
A brother, Lionel Fogarty, writes with the ink of the earth:
Am I grief in the wind/ Am I me or you and us


**6**

The earth blossoms inside a verse.

The word is born in the furrow of a history denied.

Vast territory of a hidden truth.

7

What is this country?
that gave me official citizenship,
that frames my days.
What is the truth
that denies me legal status on this land?
When the answer is the blood of genocide
that happens even now.
And this country refuses to listen to the Makarrata

8

I believe my new country is a friendship.
My new country is the struggle and dances of welcome from my
brother Steve Goldsmith.
There are stories of resistance and sharing,
voices of truth by Aunty Veronica B & Aunty Maggy
are the land of the long walk for freedom by Uncle Ken Buzzacott.

9

What is this country
Without poets or freedom fighters?
Narungga/ Ngarrindjeri, Maralinga/ Anangu

10

I am a freedom fighters' poet
writing in two colonizer languages.
My verses beating with the sound of the Mapudumgun
Cahuín, Pichintún, irse a las pailas, pichiruchi

*3 June 2021*

# Sometimes I don't know who I am when the sunset comes

"The poetic image [...] is not an echo of the past. On the contrary: through the brilliance of any image, the distant past resounds with echoes."
— Gaston Bachelard, *The Poetics of Space*

### I

Still remember an intimate conversation with myself:
The street was a space in the city of Santiago.
Where my body lived what was silent,
what lived outside and inside of me.
They were words that echoed questions,
that were thrown like stones into the water of the lagoon,
that every splash of water on the stone was a sinking question,
until today I do not know the answer from that age of the absent father.

### 2

I dig into the wounded memory—
that question that I resisted so many times before embracing it in words,
that translate all the happiness of having been there,
standing like a soldier in Moscow's Red Square—
with other compañeros who I should not name, for two reasons,
We each used political names in a clandestine political situation.
Also, our identity was an intimate space, a time of what we will be forever
I remember it was a snowy winter morning, 1982,
a motionless and ceremonious ocean invited us to be there,
facing the sun that warmed our dreams of the Bolshevik revolution.
We went down to the mausoleum with the language of silence
with echoes of the fallen. in thousands of distant and victorious battles;
I imagine myself a Condor reaching the top of the Andes Mountain range
willing to fly and fall
willing to fly and fall
willing to free the space drowned in the blood of so many.

## 3

In Australia my home is a blank page where I sit with my verses.
In deep conversation, the past is still a poem to be written.
My garden not only gives fruit to eat, as in the leaves of a cauliflower.
my verses find a home to dream.
In the broccoli florets I can read a verse from Judith Wright:
*this morning I have abandoned the garden.*
In Australia, my home, I stand on the steps of Parliament house
with a few poems from Lionel Forgarty, Ali Cobby-Eckermann
and Robbie Walker, the poet whose fate is told in the Deaths in
      Custody report.

# This afternoon I'm a character in Fyodor Dostoyevsky

*A novel is a work of poetry. In order to write it, one must have tranquility of spirit and of impression.*
— Dostoyevsky

Rummaging in the papers of the author, I'm made of codes.
My blood is a river of words, stones singing in time,
frozen in that Moscow winter visit 1982 ...

I
My eyes are footprints on the road bordering the swaying waters.
My skin an image of a dry leaf swimming
in the reflection of rays of the day and the evening—
penetrating the mind of Fyodor (pages already written in 1870).
I return home through the streets that push me towards the author.
Developing the conflict of the climax is essential.
Nothing belongs to me.
I'm again a reading in waiting.
Every night I open the pages I am there
palpitating in the heart of the reader...But where is the beating of
my own heart?
In what line or literary image do I die?
Until tomorrow... But which tomorrow will open the page marked
yesterday?
And continue the reading of the character I am.
Pain and passion were the resurrection of life
read by someone, not myself,
who gives me the freedom to be, in reading,
yet imprisons me in reality.

II

My brother was not a Karamazov, his name is Carlos.
But I baptise him in my reading: Ivan.
Distance is not absence, only moon, dark lady, howling.
Flowers for the dead
on the streets of what we were when warmed by agony.
Today I am a character responsible for that final kiss
my lips nested, dried blood that I don't even breathe today.

III

About the novel.
It is there between the written papers and cast aside by my
fatigue.
 Paragraphs... (agony of the word) in the ashes of cigarettes
whispering at the dead.
 Ink... (on stained paper) blood or cold sweat in the soul.
Chapters (abandoned from the novel) the heart is spring invaded
(invaded spring)
 by steel birds torching dreams...

Poetry... (smoke of the afternoon) character sitting in the
dreamed garden
murmuring the dialogue of Raskolnikov.

Translated by Tamryn Bennett/ Publicado en la revista *ERZA*- US
(Volume 11 Number 2)

# Lenin & Dictatorship in Chile-1988

*To Lenin Garrido*

A childhood torn, words silently
raised above that nest of hungry crows: the dictatorship in Chile.
The light in his eyes grew to shine without crossing the Andes.
His years stagnated in a pool without any echo of the absence
reflected in his childhood journals.


I tear at that piece of history
he carries inside without knowing how to love it.
That bite of pain, tasting on the skin like the depths
of a melody that doesn't yet end,
like strumming the chords of a song that doesn't feel lost.

Your words come to me like waterless rivers,
steeped, instead, in hollows of stars pain.
What identity is it that takes root
in a heart beating with love
to be thus able to love what we have,
 distancing us from what we have been,
in this reality that binds us.

# Faust: and now, here I am what I am, and I don't think I am something else

I think I'm writing
a poem about nothing, for no one.
I do not know whether I should start making a hole in the blank
page
and dig, so that the verses will appear,
or burn the sun in that line that someone wrote
on the wall riddled with bullets, blood, and a corpse;
riddled with abandon and loss of everything.

In that bombed city,
which appears from time to time while I'm reading with a coffee
or in the yawn of the news.
At dusk I start flying wrapped in the blanket
of a nightmare, of the days spent walking
in my broken shoes, worn from travelling but getting nowhere
without entering a doorway or looking through the window-frame
of dawn.

*Tonight, I found a place to sleep,*
a piece of furniture dragged by the hurricane waters to this place.
The night is today, the night with nothing more to say.
I write this poem in a language
you do not understand, not a fucking sound, nor a fucking
pronunciation.
 I write without any reader,
not even for the blindness of Borges when I read this line:
When I write something, I have the feeling it pre-exists.

* from a sketch of 'My Faust', Act II, Scene 5, in *Selected Writing* of Paul
Valér

# I don't write verses

I drink the ink, the blood and the tears.

I drink from that wellspring of passion

where I found wounded bodies,

forgotten

thirsty

smelly from so much waiting,

in those pages

where I spill the rage that others trample, arrest,

torture or murder.

I don't write verses *cause of these wounds that bind us to the bottom*

*And break the cries of our wings"*.


*Vicente Huidobro-CANTO I-Altazor

# Ink and paper

Where the word breathes.
What the soul,
as an orchard bears fruit,
so the ink is transformed
into water of aroma and flavour, but into the blood of verse.

Water and blood, a mixture of sacred dreams.
People who come down from the silence of the moor
make the foundations of the lie tremble,
that feeds the injustice
of our peoples of the South...Marichiweo!!!!

# Letter to my Grandmother

I

When life falls into a black abyss and you cling to the light of
those innocent eyes, that come just when the fall becomes more
evident and voracious, you wake up, not knowing which streets to
take. You wake up, not knowing which streets to take. But where
are the streets? Of which city? Since when have you lived in that
city?

If the pain, the absence, is a room waiting for death and you
only remember the gutters of life, you remember the pleasant
taste of an ice-cold beer, even though you have no one to toast
with. Almost the same sensation I had when I had to savour tea
with the taste of pichi, for fifteen eternal days, every morning
incommunicado, in the prison of Rancagua 1985.

That was the taste of pain, of your absence, of the loneliness of
those days of imprisonment and incommunicado detention, by
order of the Military Prosecutor's Office of Cachapoal, VI region.

II

*I drink the absence*
*I enjoy the taste of what you left us. They are so intense that it's*
*hard to choose just one memory and drink it to the last drop. If I'm*
*the last moment of your death. I'm not afraid to pronounce death.*
*I love death since you've gone from me. I drink my drink with*
*loneliness, with lovelessness like my daughter's shadow. I live the*
*separation of what leaves us on the road as if we were looking at*
*each other in a dry river, where only the image of mud or dry dust*
*converses with me today, of you.*
*I never said it... But this question drowns me: Why did you leave?*
*Why did you sow so much absence in the fruit of love?*
*After you, I live for absence. I live for goodbyes. I live for my lips*
*without the taste of a kiss from you.*

III
La Partida...
(a la Juana Maria)
It's always hard to accept.
It's a moon leaving a ray of light at the edge of the window,
Where the drunken branches of the neighboring tree
play at jumping on the icy wind of dawn.
But you're sad and tired.  Your smile grimaces
of gloom from the burning moon that fled without you.

*17 October 2019*

# About the Chilean Uprising

The return never comes.
We are passengers in transit,
between a star
defined by yesterday.
Although the heart,
always beating,
ahead
of this paper shadow,
stuck to the walls. We are.

*Adelaide, 21 February 2020.*

# The sacred is not a consumer

The sacred is survival.
God's temple and space.

We are travellers in a time of storm.
We are prisoners of the crisis
of what we define for freedom.

Back to break loose from what we consume?
We sow in the womb of Mother Earth

The sacred is not a consumer.

*2015*

# Was Nicanor Parra the King Lear of the Chilean Literary Kingdom

*Truth, is like beauty, is neither created nor lost. Nicanor Parra.*

I read King Lear as if he were here these days.
I wonder: it was Nicanor Parra, King Lear,
who translated himself using the Parrian style
as a dialogue on his deathbed, of those lands of power
in the old region of the anti-poet, even without having won the
Nobel Prize.
In any case, Shakespeare himself says, in Lear's voice:
Give me the map there.
Know that we have divided in three our kingdom.

I have been informing myself through letters, articles and opinions
about his death, on that map of Cartagena that divided his kingdom

Like blood on the streets, sword of sharp words and insults that come
and go.
Finally, I listen to what Raúl Zurita says, who was close to Nicanor.
He was the one who de-polished map lines and knew who could be
the new King Lear
from the Chilean literary domain.
By the way, I enjoyed reading Parra's King Lear Spanish translation.
Daughters of mine tell me
(Since we have resolved / leave the government territories and
concerns of the State /
Which one of you three loves us the most?

# When I die

I want next to me my verses.
Let them go with me
to that recondite space.
From being dust or memory.
Only instead of flowers and crowns,
write me unpublished poems or a single verse,
not necessarily about me, but of something that remembers
who I was or will be in you.
When I die
I want it on my gravestone.
Write a verse that nobody remembers,
those that I wrote when I was clandestine
and fire was made, ash from the raid.
When I die
I do not want tears or crying,
but rain, birds and farewell greetings.
When I die
I want everyone to carry luggage,
suitcases, bags, backpacks to cheat death,
making believe that we are all travelling
towards a place of ours.
When I die
I want you to read a paragraph of the Communist Manifesto,
or Marx's Capital.
And the hymn is humming: The Internationale
like a murmur of voices on the march.
When I die, I want to be happy for the last time, body and soul.

# Allow me to remember a Neruda Love Sonnet that I read one day in April 1979

*To Anisa Mandaula.*

Old verses are fragrances, asked questions, read dust off the soul
of Neruda and Mistral.*
Refill your poetic dream-mobile while waiting at Newcastle
Airport, the flight anchors your
trip. I go back to the city where I came from. I climb a skyward
flight. A wing grows in me,
body across the window, a long steel wing. He ties himself with
the shade and light of the
arm and the hand that writes.

Your questions breathe from language, the sound is entangled.
Verses by R.M. Rilke that come from your gaze, I read and read
again.
I think the answer that flutters in the soul, rolls along like an
apple that falls from a kiss of Esenin.*
To Isadora. I drink the flavour of Jorge Tellier's translation in
that bar in Lautaro town.*

I recite from drunken memory. I know I'm no longer a dialogue
of clouds between
past and reality. Take off or land under the lights of the eternal
city of waiting. Water of
small mirrors between skin and heartbeat. I receive your hug like
these verses that I write.

Moon and sun anchored in the oblivion of a thought. Your
questions are roots entering on the
waiting, maybe a garden where your questions bloom. Tell me, is
reality a love poem? Or

just wind embracing the birds of your humanity, bearing the
name: Anisa Nandaula.

*2019*

* Grabriela Mistral, a Chilean poet.
* Sergei Yesenin a Russian poet
* Jorge Teillier, a poet who translated Yesenin into Spanish

# In the garden gate

I think of the Amazon jungle
in the ancestral seeds
from the grandmother-mother of the first trees
of the first fluttering birds
drinking the pure water of the falling stars

that dawn when  eyes dampened the river
and the distance could not go back
and imitate the wings of birds and animals,
to climb to the top and chat with the clouds.

The animals and insects didn't need wings to fly.
All living beings were happy.
The water was heaven and earth, swimming in the eyes of the
fish.

Today everything burns as if the fire
 will close with Amazon locks forever.

*2019*

# Whom shall I call on? Who will share with me the wretched happiness of staying alive?

I open the Yeseninian luggage of my yesterday, 1980.
I remember reading the verses of Sergei Yesenin
in a clandestine bar in Pudahuel al Poniente de Santiago.
I read the drunken image of her, Isidora Duncan, or rather then
Veronica.
That night. I thought he was dead.
Blood soaked my shirt.
From the olive jacket fell bullets of lovers, and the riflemen that I
saw.
I think red wine was filled with bullets, piercing so much pain.
As a good poet, I thought I would die of love that night.
But Mrs. Mercedes told me: *Don Samuel Lafferte, it was time to
close the boliche\*.*

The night was infiltrated with stars murmuring misfortune.
I was deaf to the mockery.
Take the last bus, as you drink the last glass till almost empty.
I, a traveler with the luggage of disappointment and grief,
who should I call? Who will share with me the unfortunate
happiness of being alive?
Drunk with verses, with a kiss dragging me towards my grave,
towards this poem that I did not write, but only today,
after 30 years, I know who I should call to have a drink
in memory of the Russian / Soviet poet Sergei Yesenin, for whom
I got drunk.

\* boliche: clandestine bar

## In search for a verse that I love ...

I am looking for the verse that revives the tenderness of a kiss
on the digital moon of your absence.
In the night like this, I disembark in your body.
I'm a memory of the shore of desire
I cannot touch, nor caress the distant
kiss that flew away when I breathed your name.

I write the verse that brings me closer to you,
from the ink or the blood of Yesenin's last verse.
The day gives me your smile back.
But still, we are strangers in the same house.

I erase the verses written in this poem.
I break the digital blankness.
I drink the ink from a bottle of Gonzalo Rojas's verse.
I break my pencil with Roque Dalton's loaded soul.
In his last clandestine poem
I return to the silence of the room where I was tortured,
in that lost city in memory.

# Miguel de Unamuno's Question to Us: Why those Lilies that the Ice Kills?

Why, Teresa, and what we were born?

The wind puts this question to the poet on his grave.
Teresa responds with rain and cold breath.
She plants a kiss on the skin and in the verse of the worm.
I, a poet from the south who will read to us,
(Unamuno may think as his final verse)
my reading will be a red carnation brought from afar.
Like reading a poem in another tongue, after 1936,
blood and death, that was what we were.
Unamuno wrote: What we were born?
I don't know.
Your question is an old nest in a rare book,
like a soul flying through time and space.
2015, I am reading ... "lirios que los hielos matan?"
And you died in 1936. (en el nacimiento de la Guerra Civil de
España).
Your question resurrected on my lips
as a saliva del gozo,
joy saliva, saliva kiss, liking my dream,
cutting these lilies, kill the ice.


That and we were both?

I do not know.
maybe we were a tree planted in the soul of the world.
We went on a cloud driven by a blind sky.
Maybe we were a small Huidobro, thinking ourselves God's love
with a star.
We went yesterday (peace war wound),

we went back years (onion in the hands of the prison nursing
creature),
we went two (self, another Unamuno),
and your blood Teresa (Love in the Mist).
We were eternal in the unanswered questions.
Only death rests on nothing.
The two were nothing in the verses,
death, forgetfulness and love, those questions.


For that, and that is everything and nothing?


Violins embrace the lament of the melody,
bleed rhythm in verse, all
verse, nothing is a line.
My reading is all nothing.

Violin regrets leaving the soul
crying rivers in strings that are caught in the war—
rivers sailing at nothing, earth as a seed fruitless.
One violin asks on / off?
A guitar singing without question?
I am life in your hands and I am nothing in your dream.
I am made of love and I'm all into nothingness.
Teresa because you were all to be dust, nothing.


Why did God make us?


God replies that the dead do not ask me
who killed Miguel de Unamuno?
Teresa or lilies?
God answers: love and I have witnesses,
my son
and its poet spirit,

since the father was out partying.


Why did God make us?

God responds angrily, means:
I did not make anyone.
Each is one old enough
to know who their parents are.
I know poets fall in love and they believe as a small god,
another dog with that bone.
Excuse me, I am God not a poet.

# Today I'm borrowed verse

The moment scatters
Motionless
I stay and go:
I am a pause
(Octavio Paz: Between leaving and staying)


I read, I hold, I carry.
I enter and voices bounce off me as air consumed
on the walls of the place.
The noise is endless.
I stay, consume myself, and drink myself.
Voices speak the instant where I am.
Full of numbers and uninhabited maps
I only have a pause.
Eternity is a borrowed verse.
I will go when time dissipates.
The heart will be stale air
on the humiliated ground,
where I write for the moment, I was.
awake with the moon ruminating in my window.
The smells of the night were intense.
I fall from the cold glass of the final embrace.
Nothing remained, the moon trapped in its version
between a verse and shades of a dawn.

Let everything happen to you: Beauty and Terror
Just keep going: no feeling is not a mistake.

Rainer Maria Rilke, *Book of Hours* (1905)

When I read these verses, I feel like I'm back in those walls
where only the wounds of terror bloomed.
The murmur of blood told a story
from a river in tears,
falling through the bars,
from my eyes to the sky
that imprisoned the open window of the world.
There I heard the song of the earth made dust,
beats of poor sparrows singing
love melodies.
Everything told me who I was, even though I did not wake up. yet
the dark pain of existence,
I only heard the voices of the torturer
that told me that I was going to remove the beauty within the
terror.
I learned there, that language is the accent of blows,
sound of wounds, and prayer of cries
for life to awaken, bloom or just lick moans
within what I am, a day like today;
on the side of those you love, or loved, and maybe you will love
not as a being but as a mistake. If learning to be error,
learn to be error of a beloved feeling.
Learn to be an error of what you hate.
Now, in reality, I go on reading these verses
Returning to them, as you remember a love already gone ... forgotten.

I have returned to them as you remember what happened on
9/11/1973.
No feeling is a mistake.

No story is wrong/
No experience is an error/
No dream is a mistake, no nightmare is a mistake.
No caress is a mistake.
No kiss is a mistake.
No poem is wrong.
No word is an error.
My wounds are no longer alone in memory.
Here my skin is wrinkled with errors ...
my feet walk on trails made of mistakes.
My heart beats past, present and perhaps future mistakes.

My blood flows from all my dumb, fallen, written or spoken errors.
I refuse to believe that love is not an error.
And that hate is the only victory for an error, too.

# The best poem of the day

It is sitting there like the worn leaf of a eucalyptus.
It is falling towards the back of the ground and drinking its
silence.
It asks you to talk with other leaves that are still on top of the
tree.

Ask them if they can give you some of that majestic look.
Maybe a little cloud kiss caught between branches and sky.
Embrace your roots with pain
and feel blessed by the deepest sound on earth.

Sit there like an orphan leaf,
close your eyes and write a verse
on that sheet that is thrown on a street,
in that rainy day gutter
leaf that transforms into a boat sailing no the uncertainty of the
day.

*2018*

# Reality/ Illusion

*reality is reality or is it just an illusion*
—Ernesto Cardenal

In this midnight naked I return to prayer.

It leaves me at a paper station

train that has already left or has not yet arrived,

to take away this poem or prayer.

I'm the only driver, engine and coal.

making this journey go.

Paper is a line, landscape and voices to converse.

Words are the illusion of verse in prayer,

believing that the poet's reality is born

or the poet in his nocturnal reality, here in his room with his lamp

that ages, like a sun among clouds of books.

Are the clouds an illusion of the poet?

Or the books are reality?

Endless readings

in those hours that die without leaving traces in reality.

Illusion is a muse that looks at me in a mirror.
So am I in front or in the reflection?

Am I before the image or just illusion learning to be who I am?


I think I'm a verse learning to read a poem of the child I lost in
reality.
I think I am a grandfather learning to pray to a flower that grows
in the eyes of my grandchildren.
I think I am a kiss learning from the illusion of the beloved in the
night without light.

# The ring and the moon

I wear this ring

made memory, before I open

the heavy gate of death.


Ring of the last sigh.

Close to farewell.

Eternity of what we are.


Ring of this full moon,

against the bitter winds

from where I kiss the beloved.

*Adelaida, 13 September 2019*

# Love

Love is a deep root in the land.
The home is a bird flying to different places
until the love finds a nest
where each egg gets ready to fly free into the infinite sky,
through the mother earth.
The universe will be a mirror of their own dreams
fluttering forever.

# where I am from, when the wind mutes my footsteps

1.

where I am from...

when the wind mutes my steps,

when the damp earth warms my blood,

when I return to the road without knowing

where I'm going to take flight

from where I am...

Will I be flight? air? or only the illusion

of falling into the waters of my destiny.

*2019*

2.

I am made of what I was.

I was born from a bird that flew,

creating an ovum inside my mother.

All the desire spilled
on the sticky lips of burning flesh,

became a cup of wine in the blood.


Yesterday, I murmured to my grandson Mohamed,

of five weeks residence on earth.

All will be well, I told him.

In my arms I covered him from cold and helplessness.

Oh no! Fernando Pessoa throws his echo onto my verses.

He leaves a mirror of syllables.

Mohamed opens his left eye.

His gaze hunts the sound of my words.

I return to the dream of what was my childhood.

# What do I wait for?

A poem of expectation,
 sit down and wait for her
making a verse from a chair.
Where do you sit?
 In the gutter of any street where he is,
or on the lawn next to the road that you left behind,
and wait without agitation, or time,
or anything that makes you feel impatient.
But the question that flutters in the soul is
for what do I want to wait?
The birth of a flower that was first seed in my hands.
A kiss that is already a cloud falling from tears.
What spilled last night when I barked at the fleeting moon, of my
night without her?

What do I wait for?
To re-converse, from my boyish innocence, with grandmother
already dead.
Expect a hug that will warm me after listening to the train,
on that walk where today only, weeds grow that confuse my heart of
beauty.

*24 May 2019*

# In the guarded darkness: reading a poem in 1976

*To the poets of the Andamio Literary Workshop & Miguel Davgnino, John Smith.*

I think—remember, first turn off the lights.
Everyone slept at home.
I lit a worn candle,
 put it next to the book still closed.
There was a curfew in Chile.
The night scared a little.
Outside Bolaño's dogs barked toward bunches of poems.
I had lost a country; I think they howled.
The shots looked like shooting stars
bouncing on the rooves.

Looking out the window, it was a big mess.
A dangerous adventure or just a shitting of fear,
when you feel a rifle pointing toward your eyes.
Then, listening to my grandmother saying:
*Juan, turn off the light and go to bed.*
It was there that I took my first action.
Clandestine,
I opened the book, *Ode to the simple man*, by Neruda.
First poem read silently
in the guarded darkness.
Patrolling the night ...
I did not dare to read the last verses:
*We will win*
Although you do not believe it,
we'll win, ... a knock on the door closed the book.
The candle was spent in its agony.
Neruda was dead, that September 23rd.

I survived the reading.

I was one of those who had participated in that Neruda workshop, that night of the curfew.

## The fear of losing touch with the mother tongue/All reality ... Enrique Lihn

w
These verses of Linh are a testament
to poets who are born
to the game of the word.
o
I was translating the sound
in that learned language and what it means,
r
opening an old dictionary
and finding it in another language,
and getting lost in that new sound,
almost like a child's language,
who does not know that virtual reality.
d
The word is devoured
and it makes us move the mouse
of that game,
creating the other reality.
s

# Of where we, the overseas Australians, belong

*John Forbes (3-The Beach)*

I find this in the last line of
walking by myself on the sandy beach,
following the soul, alert like a dog.
I can smell the question
like a bone left behind
in the reflection of sunlight in the ocean.
Waves arrive and go.
The throwing stick returns wet.
I do not know who bites or throws,
where the signs of happiness come from,
where it belongs when we bark, what we are.
Life gives us a place to be born,
but when we open so many doors, to walk out
in an instant, we lose the way back.
Maybe I'm a written verse, between other written verses,
in this continent made blood, for those who devastated
the word brought as a flag
from the unknown ocean horizon ...
Of where we, the overseas Australians, belong.

*2018*

# Respond to the Why poem by Michael Dransfield

*Why- I write poems/to trick/people into*
*thinking I'm sane/I'm through with*
*fucking art/I do it for a/reason.*
*1972.ii.4 - 1:45pm*
*—Michael Dransfield*


Hi Michael, I can't say to you now

how are you? Because you are no longer here with us.

However, your poems are still being read by many poets.

I read'why' and I feel that I have to respond it.

As a poem, without cheating, but with many reasons,

I am a poet of Latin-American background

living in this Aboriginal land since 1990.

My city is Adelaide, I guess. You were here in Adelaide

reading your poetry sometime before 1972.

Well Michael, my point about your Why

is to say I did some tricks with my poems too,

when I lived in Santiago, I did few political tricks.

No, like Raúl Zurita
 se corta la cara, se lanza ácido en los ojos

The face is cut, acid is thrown into the eyes.

I wrote my poems as Samuel Lafferte

before the secret police grabbed me,

arrested, tortured and sent me to jail.

I thought with all this that I was healthy and alive

and that my poetry would win an art prize.

But what I got was a Humanitarian Visa to live in Australia.

And years later, three of my poetry books were published

in Sydney and Melbourne.

My reason to write poetry has always been

a political/humanitarian reason, just as I love the sound,

the skin, and how the words creak

on my paper's lips, full of ink and reasons to speak.

# Sitting on this blank page

Sitting on this blank page
like looking at a white bird
trying to take flight into a white sky.
There  it is confused. Stagnant.
Unable to think with its human mind,
not knowing how to say or write a word with its wing,
without understanding how a verse is born
from there, sitting on that blank page.
The years pass like a mountain covered
  in white shadow, that someday I will draw.
Today old age is an aurora of a kiss
which I remember with passion.
But kiss and verse are two rivers,
deep and dangerous to cross,
that drown anyone who attempts the feat.

Sitting on this blank page,
try to take flight in that kiss
which today made him wake up in tears.

*18 September 2017, 3:22 pm*

# Sonnet to Shakespeare's Grave
*(Third Version)*

Shakespeare's tomb is not his abandoned body.

Bones and ashes are in this place.

The gravedigger, after the funeral, goes to the inn.

He eats and drinks with his hands still dirty and smelly.


The gravedigger goes home with a caterpillar in his jaw.

At dawn he wakes from his caterpillar sleep.

He walks with his shovel as if dragging death.

Waiting, walking towards it, among the fallen leaves.


In waiting to pray, you do not know how to pronounce

or read a sonnet of death. A bird perches

and licks the edge of the blade, as if breakfast hours are random.


Hours are made of stones, mud and water.

A sonnet winter falls to the depth of a caterpillar that was ...

A butterfly eats a leaf on the edge of Shakespeare's tomb.

# I am the poem. I mean this poem

No será lo que aún no haya venido, sino
Lo que ha llegado y ya se ha ido,
Sino lo que ha llegado y ya se ha ido.
*Trilce* (xxxiii) Cesar Vallejo

Today, according to the Mayan Calendar;
I am a poem. Who will read me?
Silence.
Who will read me in a loud voice?
Who will take my hand onto the blank paper?
Who will write on my skin, bones and wounds?
On my burnt hand or on my left lame leg?
Who will write from my dreary eyes' que *llueve poemas sin tu nombre?*

Who will open my flesh to write a verse of blood within?
And pain and hope can flourish, in the ink of a garden
for all humanity,
which has been invaded by machine-guns and the capital of cash,
war, lies and greed.

On each corner of the ruined and liberated city of Ramadi
The musician plays melodies of love.

I am the poem of peace that can give
myself
to planting peace, to stop War.
I am a poem with blood, my blood
Children's blood in Syria,
Mothers' blood in Palestine, Iraq, Afghanistan.
Fathers' blood, snow blood, land blood,
volcano blood running as *a matanza de niños Mapuches*

*Donde ancestros de hoy y ayer recuperan tierra y historia.*
Blood death, blood blossom
*Primavera muerta, sol muerto*
*Luna herida, luna muerta*

Yes, Am I the poem? ...I asked my friends
I don't need to be Altazor's creator or Trilce's creator.
Each one imitates the power of God or being with God.

I prefer being a humble trucker on the colonized, invasion land.
Searching for justice and freedom.

I am el poema *soy gruñón, enojón y malas pulgas*
I am el poema words howl stop the war,
With words praying made peace.
With words struggle resistance,
against colonization of the language of any form,
word prison,
word assimilation,
word death in custody,
raíz, raíz and aire
root, root y air
raíz and agua
root y water
raíz and suelo
root y soil
raíz and frutos
root y fruits
raíz and hongos
root y fungus
de la señora María Sabina
who had taught beat generation poets,
*lo sagrado de la tierra* y el poema.

Si, yes, I am the poem where I have to wait for my master?
The poet
May be in a park, on a bed.
May be in the TBAR- Café, at the Central Market.
May be in one of the streets of Gaza or Temuko
May be in the bullet that penetrated the flesh and the heart of a
Palestinian boy.
May be in the beautiful silhouette of the prostitute,
who waits for a poem or money in New York city.


Si Yes! I am el poema that decolonized the land of the poem
that was invaded and knew genocide since 1788.
Captain Arthur Phillip and 1,500 convicts, crew, marines and
civilians
arrived at Sydney Cove.
New diseases; new vowels and consonants were weapons of death
and genocide.


More than 500 Indigenous nations inhabited the Australian
continent,
approximately 750,000 people in total.
Their cultures had developed over 60,000 years, making
Indigenous Australians the custodians of the world's
most ancient living culture.
Each group lived in close relationship
with the land and had custody over their own traditional country.
 Long live the Warriors!!
Long live the Resistance Warriors!!
Long live the Freedom Fighters Warriors!!

I am el poema, but the real poem writing with ink in love,
with ink speak of space nature, space for a bird, space for a spider.
I like to be el poema, barking to a butterfly of death,
barking to the hot north wind,
riding on the Great Ocean Road,
barking to the moon and sending paz y justicia
to my friends at Manus Island and Nauru Concentration Camp.
Please let them be a bird on this land, said the poeta.

Yes! I am el poema, somebody has to write, read and feel it.
Where is the poet? Who is it? Where are they?
Where do they come from?

Where is the poeta?
Can I make it; I mean the poet.
*No será lo que aún no haya venido, sino*
*Lo que ha llegado y ya se ha ido**

*30 December 2015*

*Cesar Vallejo's *Trilce*, a book by the Peruvian poet

# Life is still walls and blood on black dream skin

*For Robert Walker and 450 Aboriginal people who died in the Deaths in Custody System in Australia.*

Life is still walls and blood on black dream skin,
arriving but never landing on the shore of who they are.
Before the first shooting, not of a kangaroo, but of a blackfella,
the invasion: the sound of harsh translation into their own
understanding of humanity.
Robert Walker, poet; one of a long list of deaths in custody.
His words a howl outside and inside the prison where he perished.
His verses were as yet open wounds, or in Language, the vowels
for dreams of freedom.
His consonants were the rhythm of brutality against his people.
I found him in a second-hand book place.
I read his poem's lines: Have you ever begged for blankets
From an eye staring through a hole in the door*.
The poet wrote these verses, a testimony of lock up.
Blood and land are still mourning for justice and freedom.
Have you ever spent 30 years waiting in a roll call
at the Deaths in custody Royal Commission?

# We are birds without light

*Eternal and old youth that has left me unnerved:*
*like a bird without light*
*Letter of Homero Aldo Expósito (1944)*

We are birds without light,
learning to be, and not to be, in the valley of the past.
Repetition of wings escaping from the shadow of the day.
We are wings flapping letters, words.
Cries trampled on the bitterness of suffering.

Maybe we are a tango, closure of moons,
bodies dancing to dark,
breathing to the beat of the bandolón in the skin.
All my life is yesterday: it stops me in the past.
Heartbeat of a kiss falling from yesterday.
And it touches all those who gave us suffering
in that cell number 86.
What made me go anywhere?
We only cultivate freedom, like a bird without light

Today I sing this tango as a cry for love of yesterday.

*29 December 2017*

# Today call death by its name

*to those who*
*Inside and outside*
*they live and they go out of their way*
*they die and they are destroyed*
*The House and The Brick Mario Benedetti**

Today call death by its name.
I have it here. It sends me official documents or
romantic letters, telling me that it wants to kiss me
or that it will soon destroy me.
I no longer write a single word in response.
I prefer to use my ink
which is sometimes water or blood,
that falls through empty papers
and wets it with so much human crying,
with so much crying, fallen to earth.
But my ink is water or blood, made up as paper.
The word that falls on the paper sometimes
do not know how to pronounce the wounds,
those similar wounds that are shaken from debris every day.
I go back to my home, I mean, to the poem
that awaits me without time, without condition.
It awaits me, hugs me.
It makes me happy as the kiss of ink and paper,
like a kiss on my body, defeat
in my surviving body, dead and loved.
I call my poem my home:
poem built like the bricks of Mario Benedetti
without a door, because to enter in
I must walk endless paths,
use shortcuts that get lost in my veins
and fall to the heart of the moment I lived or I love.
I enter the garden to work with the roses and its thorns,

blossomed during this time of such cruelty.
There I go next to one of my windows
that gives me the immensity of the ocean,
that same ocean where the tyrant (1980)
orders bodies thrown, tied to the death-torturer
on pieces of rail cut by murderous hands.
Oh, dear names / which I name from time to time
as a conversation or fresh ocean foam beer
that makes me talk with the living memory—
that which brings fire,
that cooks a meal of friends,
who survived so much evil.
I told you that I enter the poem,
my true home,
the only one that I have, mine,
since everything else is rent,
it's money, it's payment, it's debt or private service or purchase...
I told you that I enter the poem,
my home, that's for sure. I'm sitting at my table
when I read old Benedetti.
We talk over a bottle of red wine
of stale verses, words and loves.
That's why, when I go back,
                            and someday it will be
I will be here old dear poet,
waiting for you
in our home, common as the poem should be.


* Mario Benedetti, an Uruguayan poet

# Listen to the other sound on this blank line

Listen to the other sound on this blank line
Escucha, solo escucha lo que quise decir
I am sitting here
Murmurando lo que vendrá
Waiting for a sign to talk
Queriendo escribir lo que aún no tengo
I know. I feel all the tiredness on my body's planet
Llego aquí como un solo cuerpo, mi mano es movimientos
del océano,
I can feel my hand fighting so hard to write even this word
in the ocean
Mis dedos del pie izquierdo es una roca expulsada del mar
My left feet scratched the wet rock at the shore of the sea
Y mi mente sentada ahí donde ningún habitante la espera
encontrar
But my mind is the only inhabitant in the desert that I call your
absence

Creo que soy yo quien al final del camino desanda este poema
contra el tiempo.
I think it's me who, at the end of the road, retraces this poem
against time.

*January 2018*

# What to do when you lose faith?

*Dedicated to my dear friend Sr. Janet Mead*

Go home, make yourself a cup of tea.
Break the left foot of the man on the cross
So, you can reinvent the sacred trinity.
Instead of the old spirit, leave in its place
a certain Oscar Romero.
Let the son go from heaven to the earth.
And live with an Indigenous community.
Let the father, whether biological or otherwise,
find work again to give a better life to his flock.
Let the prayer be a seed, rather than words,
May it be sown as potatoes, onions, and corn.
May the Lord's Prayer no longer be so much ours
But a million copies of Sister Janet Mead's song.
And be played again as a modern rock hit
Not in churches, but in schools and in shopping centers
Let it be declared a subject of music and literature
From elementary school onwards.
Religion should no longer be seen as Karl Marx's opium
but rather as an honest conversation
between Fidel Castro and Frei Betto,
So that our dead, those who gave their all for a better world
Become living stars, verses by Ernesto Cardenal
Former minister of the Sandinista Revolution.
May the song: Our father, sung by Sr. Janet Mead
Finally, be sown in the earth
Like a melody of social solidarity and revolution
of that creed so much tampered with for ever and ever. Amen.

# 2

# New political poems

"The old world is dying, and the new world struggles to be born:
now is the time of monsters."
"El viejo mundo se muere. El nuevo tarda en aparecer. Y en ese
claro oscuro surgen los monstruos"
—Antonio Gramsci

# Scott Morrison vs Anthony Albanese

After the Howard dynasty and its little imps,
I think we will return to breathe the scent of the eucalyptus
wet by the May rain.
Maybe we will not be paper thrown to the dreams of our destiny.
Let freedom no longer be a boat sinking in human pain,
numbers of cruelty statistics.
I vote for suffering humanity. I vote for an ancestral seed.
I vote for the detention walls to be finished.
I vote for the homeless to end, for the language of mother earth to
open our soul.
I vote for the peaceful resistance of who we are
in the heart of the child, that grows in death in custody's prison.

# The consciousness of the park is dryness

*For Behrouz Boochani and Janet Galbraith*

We are citizens wounded in the heart.
There are other citizens injured by the genocidal story that does
not end.
Others have left in the corner of a space that denies life and
dreams.
Although, stubbornly, it is they who continue to create life and
dreams
for humanity.
We know their names:
here in the cities, the form of oppression
has the flapping wings of the Magpie,
cities that leave us the taste
of the groundwater of injustice,
where we only peck at the thirst,
with the illusion of rain that does not arrive.

The consciousness of parks is dryness,
and makes us dream about the deserts of apathy,
that give the moment over to believing we fly free.

*17 August 2018*

# An urgent poem you should edit from your heart, not…

War is a dirty business.
The Yankees want to be judge and executioner of the planet.
Freedom is a cell of consumption and wealth.
The media
are the chemical weapons of power
burning our soul,
leaving us voiceless,
compelling us to listen with horror to their lies,
as if the truth were fabricated with the Pentagon and its allies.

The media create a false market of invasion, death and
destruction.
Then I ask myself: Where is the old peace bastard
trying to win the corrupt prestige of the Nobel Academy?
Or waiting in the official corridors for some other rulers
to negotiate another kiss or medal for his crown?

My verse is a shot on the page that is bled
in the streets invaded by lies and oppression,
for those cities of corrupt power:
Washington D.C, Canberra, London, Riyadh & Tel Aviv

*8 April 2017*

# Maralinga atomic weapons diabolically sound Hiroshima

*It is September 27, 1956. At a dusty site called One Tree, in the northern reaches of the 3,200-square-kilometre Maralinga atomic weapons test range in outback South Australia, the winds have finally died down and th countdown begins. Liz Tynan Senior Lecturer and Co-ordinator Research Student Academic Support, James Cook University*

I do not know if I want to continue writing.
I do not know if I want more verses that adorn words
of the predators of evil and those who extirpate the roots of the
earth—
the raptors, criminals against humanity,
those who poison our mind,
those who programmed terrorist drones against other countries,
those who applied the anti-terrorist laws,
to tyrannise the Mapuche ancestral lands,
old tyrants and their accomplices of political, academic and literary
silence.
Even an international tribunal does not sentence them,
not even put them a second in jail, or sentence them through popular
justice.
Today it is raining outside.
I want to drink these verses of rain.
Let my soul get wet
so my skin, bones and blood
turn into sticky, useless mud,
that leaves me without air,
without anything, there in the dry, lifeless soil
and banish to oblivion everything
I loved, and even what I love today.
I want to be, and make myself, raindrops
falling, sliding down my bare skin
falling through my eyes. No matter that they think I cry,

because I'm crying,
because I'm falling, here where the garden is born,
where they leave their dry leaves, wet, almost dying
between branches of a bare tree in front of nothingness.
Because each one of us has turned this place into nothing
yes, this tree, pruned and without leaves and buds,
that expects the fruits of that spring to come,
that doesn't announce yet,
that is beyond feeling, of vision without heaven,
of its wet touch and in agony.

I am and I will be just rain, mud, and puddles of dirty water
in front of the door, not of Dante, nor of Borges,
nor of this garden,
where the wet hens waiting cackle for food.

I am and I will be just rain, making mud in my dreams
where I am a naked tree embraced by wind and water,
falling into the depths of the abyss, and it is impossible for me to
dig anymore.

Philosophers have hitherto only interpreted the world in various ways; the point is to change it. Karl Marx 1845 Theses on Feuerbach

Without the practice of sports,
climbing, being in prison,
would they have occurred:
the Assault on the Moncada Garrison,
its revolutionary example,
the preparation of the Granma expedition,
the clandestine meeting between Che and Fidel in Mexico
and the triumph of the revolution?

Fidel banished illiteracy with a people of pencil, paper and conscience;
The new person was born and universities multiplied.
Batista's reality was transformed into songs of Revolution
inspired by the poet José Martí to a group of guerrillas coming down from the mountains
and giving US Imperialism a headache, as Roque Dalton said.
Fidel was educated in Martí,
a visionary, persevering and courageous disciple.
He read the beating heart in the apostle's thoughts.
Fidel resolved the contradiction of bourgeois power
only 228 miles from the Empire.
638 times they tried ... it is a Guinness record for assassination attempts.
His answer was to build Socialism.
Socialism, where to be poor is to be a creator of equalities,
solidarity, brotherhood
with the humblest of the earth.

Fidel's thought became medicine, science,
reflection on the issues that harm humanity.
Your ideas are sown as a daily nourishment
of what it takes to make a new world possible.

Cuba is humanity in the deep soul-verse of Jose Martí.
Cuba is humanity in the thousand battles of ideas by the Eternal
Comandante.

## To reduce the presence of darkness in my life....
## Italo Calvino

Last Saturday evening
I awakened when Calvino allowed me to read that line.
I heard in the news the lockdown will be suspended at midnight.
Thanks, God, for only seven days of encierro.

My room in that evening was full of sun.
Sleeping on top of my bed unable to run
across my own blank East, looking
to embrace her beautiful West flesh.

At my window, I hear the rain howl
with a broken red bottle falling
like dark tears through the curtains,
wetting my verses written on that night.

# Front line

The heart is filled with hot blood
where the bullet points to the eye,
to the body and to history.
Barricades that cut
that clouds and sinks our life in misery.
These kids grew up, fought the shit.
These kids grew up, gathered rage like a dry river.
These kids grew up, the best of our wounds,
of those who fell in combat from the resistance.
The front line
is not verse, nor song, nor dance.
It's revolution that is here and stays
to defend what they wanted to torture, riddle and disappear
in this long and wide territory of fear, sown by the scoundrels of power.

# Okay, shut up poetry …

*Night, maker of enchant….*
*and if I sleep, I don't feel what I live …*
—Lope de Vega

Okay, shut up poetry …
yes, in my homeland death
is made by bullet, torture and rape.
You ask me: why don't I use a metaphor?
I answer: because the night kills,
because the eyes cry blood.
Inside is the hollow crack of the shot.
The State is the terrorist and the culiaos pacos*.

Dry blood in the streets or on the walls.
It has names of rebel citizens,
lists of wounded, without eyes,
bleeding hearts,
until the open wound is never a law
of the 80's Constitution of Pinochet.

\* Fucking police

# I Pray

*So, I pray, under /*
*The sign of the world's murder, the ruined son;*
*Why are you silent?*
—Daniel Berrigan

We have lost the seed of the soul on earth.
I am planting it.
I harvest it
to eat at the communal table.
We, the citizens living in a time of conflict,
our language is a menu to survive life.
Our heart becomes a cruel time clock.
Heavy blows are  daily work hours.
We are barefoot beggars in an economic system.


The tragic beauty of the face of Christ shines in our hearts*
We refuse to see it.
Tears of Nauru are nothing.
Then, smoking a cigar in the streets
or drinking a beer at the local pub,
pain, a cold food like garbage, left no compassion.
Compassion prayer.
We no longer have time to confess.
Our soul and mind are too busy to confess our daily sins.
Compassion, bread and old wine.
Waste in the temple of worship of money and power.
What has become of root system thirst for happiness?
Our bread is an autumn leaf tossed into the branches, as the bird
dies.
They make wine from the waters of these rivers,
suffering, bloodied by the veins of Syrian children.
Wine is the blood of indifference on the streets of Palestine.
The wine is the blood of cruelty in Nauru ... Why are you silent?

Therefore, I pray
as an old Communist, crucified on the iron bed;
nailed by electricity and blows in 1985 in the House, Borgoño.
I don't pray for those men who killed, raped and destroyed our
coexistence.
In the name of God
they crucified our bodies as agony on earth.
They poisoned our dream.

Silence. For 24 hours, a communications satellite operated
between us and God.
Praying is no longer a simple and humble action for peace.
Now it is a lost habit using a prepaid mobile phone,
instead of a plan for peace on earth.
I pray against the multinational company that devours our will.

I pray that the goodness of our hearts becomes actions.
Resisting the apathy of those who see the homeless as invisible
things in a park.
I pray that one day in my street,
we have a feast of joy and community, on the empty paths,
where rubbish bins pretend to be trees astonished by new
relationships.
Children giving flowers to strangers.
I pray, with the broken dream of a child in the Nauru Detention
Center.
But at dawn it will open our hearts, like a door of compassion
and goodness will be a meal to share in this country.

I pray, for a rebel spirit.
It can be a seed planted in the earth
and be with us in our daily struggle for peace.

*This line is part of a Daniel Berrigan poem.

# rhythm is born of nobody; they throw it naked and crying

*'Classic Acode', Gonzalo Rojas*

I speak of Gaza.
Death is born there.
They start walking,
they confront it and shoot it.

The air in Gaza is whipped.
Bullets penetrate
the crying rhythm, says the poet.

I speak of Gaza crying.
I wash my tears in  contaminated water.
I read a poem with the light off
at the table where they watch over death.

I speak of Gaza naked.
With the cold embracing me, full of love.
The kiss of death.
It hurts, on the edge of so much evil.

*17 May 2018*

# Page 47, if Homer had come to visit Australia

*Your hearts never lifting with any joy*
*You've suffered far too much.*
—Homer; *Circe and Cyclops.*

In the corner of this political crisis
I can see through a boat that reached the shore of our hearts.
They are near secure borders.
Even any seagull can fly in or out,
carrying any message from the Manus detention center.

At the corner of the PM's official words
cruelty is our own secure border.
embracing the dark waves of uncertainty.
Humanity is no longer a common ground.

I'm reading page 47; I think if Homer had come visiting
this morning to Australia, embarking on these lines:
Your hearts never lifting with any joy.
You've suffered far too much.
I continue reading his invitation to land here:
but come now, eat your food and drink your wine
till some courage fills your chests,

until our lives and hearts are mended
with the food of compassion, courage and wine,
to celebrate the nation of a fair go for all.

I am reading page 47; I believe that if Homer had come visiting
Australia this morning
embarking on these lines:
Your hearts never lifting with any joy.
You've suffered far too much.
I continue reading his invitation to land here:

but come now, eat your food and drink your wine
till some courage fills your chests.
And our lives and hearts will be mended
with the food of compassion and courage's wine,
to celebrate a nation's fair, go for all.

# Who shot Camilo Catrillanca?

Who shot Camilo Catrillanca?
It was the antiterrorist law applied from Pinochet.
It was the Jungle Comando trained in the Colombian tropics
with the collaboration of the United States and Chilean politicians.
It was the four police members of the Jungle Command,
shedding blood on the Wallmapu,
shooting the Mapuche warrior Weychafe.*

who was going back home driving a tractor.
He tilled the land and built his house with his hands and his
ancestral dreams at sunsets,
land recovered by his Temucuicui community.
There was the Weychafe with a bullet in the head
and his blood spilled on the earth.
His eyes are stuck in the beams of his house, to build
walls of love massacred,
fallen space of dying love,
as roof of sky and stars to protect
the lives of their children.

Who shot Camilo Catrillanca?
Who are those monsters armed with hate, thirsty for blood?
Shooting to kill, not knowing that if they kill him.
His soul is a seed in the blood of their ancestors, who sow in the
eternal waters of love.

*Weychafe: Guerrero/Warrior

# Organic Tomatoes for John Howard

Memory refuses to turn to dust or nothing. They just remain there like old papers. Nothing leaves them forgotten, they are there, they remain there, testimonies of days and moments that are nailed to the walls of this daily history. That day John Howard PM visits the city of Adelaide, rumours create more rumours, that we should do something, to show our rage against him, that he is coming to the Tandanya Aboriginal Cultural Centre.
Word spreads to wait for him with a protest.

Someone shouts over there! Here comes the official car turning, from Hutt St. onto Wakefield St., right at the traffic lights, the eggs crack on the back glass of the car, the empty carton flutters like a frightened bird, in the image of the frightened face, behind the smudged glass.
I cross the street and the police follow me. They make a security cordon, there are already hundreds of protesters shouting against Howard.

The police approach me and ask: What do you have in your bag? I answer with another question: Why? And I said: I have a book, a notebook and tomatoes.... but very tasty organic tomatoes.
One of the policemen tells me: NO. Don't you dare throw it. I say to myself: Why not? They've already thrown eggs at him.

Weeks later I read in the local newspaper that they had passed an 'offence law' against those who throw eggs or tomatoes at the authorities.

Late at home, I prepared a very tasty meal of tomatoes, garlic, onions and scrambled eggs.
John Howard never knew, that in an Adelaide home, a family of refugees were sitting around the table sharing a delicious meal.

## 'I'm going to Salvador Allende, the walkers say...' Eduardo Galeano

We were a tragedy created by USA-CIA.
Nixon and Kissinger the horror strategists of "11 September" .

In the streets of the town,
on those ceilings that were the anteroom
of eyes announcing flames, fire
bursts and shadows of evil,
in that Santiago of 1973.
They were forbidden parks.We pecked like birds against the walls of
oppression.
We were bleeding in the crust of death.

Sometime later, 1976, came the street theatre.
 We went out like love puppets,
undressing fear, in that amateur actor dialogue.
Through the streets, churches and unions,
courage was staged at the moon.

The hidden smile came out again
behind the windows of so many break-ins,
soldiers shot at the sunsets of September.

We were the re-incarnation of Juan Rulfo in that Santiago of 1973.
I remember when I read: 'Comala',
It wasn't just reading, we talked,
between dead and alive.
The pain was truncated spring.
'Every sigh is like a sip of life that one gets rid of' *

*11 September 2019*
*\*Juan Rulfo- Pedro Paramo.*

# Reflection about my Australian citizenship

I

Before leaving I thought: When I am a citizen of another
ancestral land.
Then it was that I landed in Sydney as a Condor with wings
bleeding.
I walked on the streets of Adelaide with the defeated flights
of that Condor, that I was.

II

My language was to open and close old suitcases
where everything was, that had fed my soul.
This was the beginning of communication.
They invited me to pronounce my origin and my verses
in the language of genocide.

III

Then I learned that the ancestral inhabitants of this land,
as citizens, were recognized,
from this continent of more than 80,000 years of existence,
in that 1967 referendum. When I was still a 10-year-old boy.
I was a child playing at being a bird trying to cross the Andes.
And today I walk, after so much resistance and defeat.
They are my brothers who give me an open heart.

IV

When speaking, I have the shadow accent of a kangaroo on my
walk.
I jump with a lame leg and I still try to take flight,
jumping in the attempt to reach the defeated wings of my inner
condor.
So, I do not know if this accent of language
is an eternal struggle of being in the word.

V
I understand who I was at birth.
I try to decolonize that exile and make the word new.
An open verse full of water beats
on the river where my verses sail after so much emigration.

# Verse or seed for peace against the War Market

I give you a verse or seed for peace.
This is a small verse
like a seed to plant
not on contaminated soil
not in the land sown with the dead
of wars of merchants.
Small verse to sow in your heart.
Clean, fresh and open for a cosmos flower in autumn.

I am an old poet, militant, not so old either,
believer of peace in revolution
like a sweet and loving kiss
of life created for the simple verses or little one
like peace.
Simple or small verse but ardent against death
who has come to glorify the war.

# 'I am the size of what I see'

*Alberto Caeiro-Fernando Pessoa- Book of Restlessness*

*All my gratitude and friendship to Ernesto Cardenal, Gloria Gabuardi, Francisco de Asís Fernández, Luz Marina Acosta, Álvaro Rivas, Elvis Hernández and Dieter Stadler.*

Managua, July 17. 10.30 am

I'm on my way to Ernesto Cardenal's house.

They pick me up at the 'Hotel Villa Americana',

the poet and friend of Don Ernesto, Luz Marina.

I think I'm awake. Very awake,

after breakfast at Café de los Poetas.

The city is Florida.

Crowns are exchanged for US dollars in the streets.

We enter the corner of the market, the light changes.

Today is my last visit to Ernesto Cardenal.

I feel a lightning nest in my blood.

He had two little questions in his pocket.

I didn't find the piece of paper.

Maybe I lost it in some corner of the house,

the streets or the hotel room.

Cardenal instead signed his books for me,

with the friendship of verse and humble prayer.

Much later, I remembered the questions. on the plane to Havana.

Where do the poets or prophets of our time hide, in the temple of technology?

What is your opinion about intimate time, that social time which is part of universal

existence?

Luz Marina, (president of the House of the Three Worlds)

of beautiful Granada,

tells me: Maybe the poet hates time, is sullen with time.

On the other hand, I think that time for Ernesto Cardenal,

(Priest, former Minister of Culture of the Sandinista Government,

Community member of Solentiname Island

and Prophet of 'The Gospel in Solentiname')

means days of reading about the universe and the resurrection, about the daily life of Joseph and Mary, through the streets of the world.

Hours— lightning days hammering the silence in the verse,

prayer on the pages of waiting.

Weather: -schedules, visits, signs of hours slipping away.

The modern suffering of the resurrection of what we are not yet.

We're just bloodstained nails in the old timbers,

of that old construction, of the oppressive system

that governs us for centuries and centuries.

Jesus has been betrayed for ever and ever.

Jesus was and will be a riddled revolutionary;

like Allende, Che and Gaddafi.

So who betrays the revolution?

The poet has seconds of stars, reading the agony of the flesh,

minutes of the cosmos, in reading,

recreating, the true resurrection of mankind.

Agony of daily life,

where the streets have rivers of blood

and the trees contain bomb nests.

Few questions the system, says Italo Calvino.

They say that in the twin cities there is no longer any way

of knowing who is alive and who is dead.


 Today I know that Managua, where the poet lives, who transforms

the inhabited verses, the hours of the human Cantico.

It's time to say goodbye.

Outside, the noise, the closed door,

where the whistle is no longer bells,

but a whistle hanging around the poet's neck.

Sounds, I say goodbye, thank you our father.

(Fragment of a long poem)

*July 2019*

# God Bless America

*Dedicated to President Nicolas Maduro and the People of Bolivarian Revolution*
*"Control the food*
*And you will control people;*
*Control oil*
*And you will control the nations;*
*Control the money*
*And you will control the world"*
*(Henry Kissinger 1973).*


When the war drums of the US sound
I mean, they're coming: death, invasion, and hunger.
Dictators will come in civil dress or military uniform.
The Condor plan is coming.
The phantom of Pinochet, Somoza, the 'Juntas Militares' of South America.
I get old names: Henry Kissinger, Richard Nixon,
and now that Trump.
The massacre of Libya, Syria or Iraq.
Still I can see the image of the young man that I was (1973).
Above the roof of my house in flames, fire and smoke.
Bombing La Moneda,
where Compañero Presidente Salvador Allende was killed.
It comes to me on September 11, 1973.
The howl, rifle butts, kickback, the shots, the blood, come to me,
of dead people in the streets, in the rivers, in the stadiums,
in my memory.
The military come to me in the streets.
The number of massacres comes to me—
30,000 Disappeared in Southern Latin America.
So much resistance from our homeland comes to me.
The speeches of Comandante Fidel come to me.
The liberation war of Nicaragua comes to me.
The Salvadoran guerrilla war.

The death of Comandante Ana María and Comandante Marcial.
News that we hear on Radio Moscow,
from the University of Komsomol.
The execution of Roque Dalton comes to me,
by his own companions, the order given by Comandante
Villalobos.
The CIA and its democratic businesses throw bodies into the sea,
 fill the rivers with blood, and increase the list of DISAPPEARED
in Chavista and Bolívar land.
 Writing this poem, God Bless America,
the news comes to me: Ernesto Cardenal
is in a serious condition in a Managua hospital.
Pope Francis raises 'suspension to divinis,'
imposed by the Vatican in 1984.
The rebel poet and priest
Ernesto Cardenal on his deathbed.
He is given his first mass,
his most humble and vigorous blessing,
as if it were his first verse of the cosmic song,
the celestial bodies / and ours. /» Walking stars »-
as if it were his first kiss-verse to Claudia.
I have so many encounters in the clandestine life...
Writing this poem: God Bless America.

# Julian Assange's Prison Cell

You. We are all vigilant of big brother.
Your voice is the dry blood in the streets, when
the American soldiers shot civilians long ago.
No one remembers or accepted the widow's tears,
their children trying to pronounce the names,
in the eternal coffin of children ages.
Or the flowers at the tombs of an unknown Baghdad cemetery
reveal unclassified documents which are statistics of deaths and
destruction
of lands,
homes
and countries, perhaps suburbs smelling of an everyday life.
One day, everything was fire, death and debris
as though our lives were back to where we'd had a home long ago.

# I Am Thinking of Che ...

*The revolution is not an apple that falls when it is ripe. You have to make it fall.*
—Che Guevara


These days, these times of so much revelry of consumption,
where life becomes impossible for Guevaristas' dreams,
where depression is the only apple
chewed out of the capitalist paradise.

From my heart in pieces, I think of Che,
of his asthma, of his decayed feet
through the mud, on the path to liberation.
I think of Che in his readings, after combat.
I think of Che surrounded by fake news,
bombarding, after his last moments of existence.
I think of Che ... When I say that this humanity,
silenced, tortured, haunted, repressed, we have a duty to survive.
I think about Che when I eat an apple from my garden.
The revolution is not an apple that falls when it is ripe. You have
to make it fall.

*2019*

# Oh Syria

*History, which is a simple whore, has no decisive moments but is a proliferation of instants, brief interludes that vie with one another in monstrousness.*
—Roberto Bolaño, *2666*

I close my notebook

without any hope of a poem

and I end the reading of 'The Savage Detectives'.

I close everything I have written today.

I enter the open cellar left by Bolaño.

No water, no food, no light.

Darkness embraces the hidden cry.

I lie in that corner

where skin sweats fear.

Oh life of Syria ...

The life of a mother crying

in front of the real picture of Guernica,

through the rubble streets of Damascus

in these days of so much western barbarism.

*14 April 2018*

# Poemas en tiempos de una Guerra Anuncida...

Peace.
We are those who never live in peace,
always speak about peace,
but our life is what was planned, to make us
a wounded people.
Peace is an illusion in this world of liars,
liars and media controlling
us like a missile
that destroyed our home, city and country.
We are homeless in our country that looks on me as foreign.

*16 April 2018*

# Light and Prison

*I thought the light was mine ... Miguel Hernández*

I
Children are no longer heirs of the light.

They sleep under the fear and debris, of the war that others reported on TV.

Other children rise under of the ice of Nauru Detention Centre.

They are no longer children, they no longer have a name.

They're only finite numbers of the cruel system.

There are children waking up in the shade of the empty glass,

at the abandoned table,

play and tread vomit, blood of the war in Syria,

among debris from a nightmare

on the walls of modern Guernica of Picasso.

The mother already dead. The father trapped by his invisible walls,

drinking what the moon leaves on its way into the night.

## II

The walls do not speak of anything.

Whisker stripes on old prison walls.

That language always made me cry.

Here I bring you a beloved and forgotten verse,

a verse by Miguel Hernández.

I do not flee from you,

I look for you in Madrid, through the abandoned streets of the resistance,

those streets, that today, have corners, and bus-stops with your name.

## III

I am a verse translated by the abandonment, I have nothing,

other than what I wrote in prison.

I was an obscure monologue,

prayer of the bread loaf and the tea with pichi* flavour,

that blessed my dawn of survival in those nights,

translated by the bars of the shadows.

I am a verse that I re-read, write and erase, that oblivion without name.

I am a bilingual verse, here in this city where light is forgotten—

wings of a treeless bird, that lives in the ditches of the late afternoon,

pecking the memory of those verses that I read, long ago, from my skin.

I am a jail with a window / Before a great loneliness of roars.


*Pichi a word from the Mapudungun language and adapted to the common speak of the Chilean people.

# Mamo' Contreras died Friday aged 86

And you'll ask: Why doesn't his poetry
speak of dreams and leaves
and the great volcanoes of his native land?
From *(I'm Explaining A Few Things by Pablo Neruda)*

Fire burns and warms me.
I'm very close to the last embers of fire,
naked cold, lashing the memory of those days in the Borgoño
house.
Five intense days of torture and open wounds.
Death visited my body, spilt blood on it.
'The doctor' examined him.
'There are blows in life so hard...I don't know ... Cesar Vallejo.

He planned and created DINA.
I survived and resisted, to liberate,
as a seed hidden in the heart of Mother Earth.
The night is cold, burning embers.
Over there, morning smells of impunity, rotten power.
Burning embers are extinguished slowly.

Memory is a red carnation flourishing, in the chest that hurt in
1980.
Memory is not a tomb.
It is not an empty hole.
Memory is not only a song to sing for the fallen compañeros.
There is a Neruda verse, 1937:
'Treacherous generals
  Jackals that the jackals would despise,
   Burning embers are saying goodbye
  stones that the dry thistle would bite on and spit out,
recapture the body cold and fear
vipers that the vipers would abominate! '

23 years in Australia
'Deaths in Custody' is a long list of blood and silence.

'Deaths in Custody' is a genocide on this sacred land.
I am in pain, in anger and hopelessness,
a survivor of the evil of the Terrorist State 1973-1990.

I live in a system that tortures and imprisons us;
and now the Mapuche warriors are accused by the Anti-terrorist law
18,314.

Marichiweo,
I received news: Cristian Levinao,
entering under clandestine struggle,
after he escaped the prison,
as the winter forest galloping gave him a shelter, into the immense
snow camouflage.

Further news:
'Vigil for Mohammad Nasim Najafi, who committed suicide
in Yongah Hill Detention Centre last week'.
As his body was carried from the centre,
loaded into an ambulance under a white sheet.
fellow detainees chanted in volleys of Arabic and English:
"He did not kill himself, the immigration killed him."


Embers go, go, go.
Cold curls up on my body.
I am a survivor, one more member of the Resistance.
I'm here watching the fire die ...
I'm here tonight listening to Mamo.

With another Neruda verse
'I accuse ' Henry Kissinger, Richard Nixon, the CIA and Pinochet

of imposing the National Security Doctrine.
Mamo was believed to be a Supreme Condor, in the flight of death,
shredding bodies between the abyss and the sea.
He made iron pieces and tied them to the bodies, to be lost in the ocean.
'The pact of silence' sentenced him to 526 years in prison,
and never paid for it as a crime against humanity.

With another Neruda verse
'I accuse' Patricio Awlyin, Richard Lagos, Eduardo Frei and Michelle Bachelet
of concealing and promote 'the pact of silence' with traitor Generals and their institutions.
Nor forgiveness, nor oblivion ... justice !!!

I degraded your medals of terror.
I degraded them with the dignity and memory for those who died.
Memory is alive
in the air, stars that illuminate our struggle,
in the wine, love and freedom will be born in our land.
Today Friday 7th of August Mamo Contreras died;
I fall in love with all those who fight, resist and sing for a new humanity to be born.

# Pablo Neruda's death September 23, 1973

The death of Pablo Neruda was a funeral
in the silence and weapons trained on him to death or life?
On the streets of Santiago.
That morning,
when terror occupied the city everywhere.
In front of the chariot, dead poet.
Behind the Nobel Prize in Literature 1972.
On both sides of the clandestine life
against the other traitor, he does not deserve to be appointed.
And he chased you and lost your trail in Andes mountains 1946*.

The soldiers stood at the corner of La Chascona **
in each ditch where people stood, with courage
to say goodbye to our Comrade poet.
I grew up writing poetry during the 'curfew'.
Neruda, my poems were leaves of those hidden nights,
against weapons of death pointing toward your name.

*La Chascona was the house of the poet in Santiago
**Neruda went into exile through the Andes mountains when the Traitor
Gonzalez Videla sentenced him (1946)

# More than alone on the shore of the ocean…
# here in Australia

*More than alone on the shore of the ocean*
*I give myself like a wave*
*To the monotonous transmutation*
*Of water into water*
*Myself into myself*
—Paul Valéry

1

More than alone on the shore of the ocean…Here in Australia

the shore gets mixed up with blood,

boats licking cries and fears,

waves-bodies

waves-eyes

waves-tears

waves-despair.

At the shore I don't see eternity any more.

I hear voices drowning in our waves of apathy.

2

I give myself like a wave...

myself as a long desert,

myself as the sand of a dead road. With no turning.

I have prints on the shore that wet the night.

And a dream comes here in a wave.

I only have this dream,

I was almost dead and I was sailing on the ocean

like a hunter of horizons

# Listening to the Song: The Garden Went into The Sea by Mikis Theodorakis, Odysseus Elytis

*Dedicated to the Nauru and Manus detainees*

Rose and sea gave us melodies.
A rose lives on the shore like an abandoned boat.
Howls and waves wet her body.
Wounds, sand, trodden pieces of seashells and tears
left from Mother Earth.

A wet rose wave coming to kiss its petals.
And again, asks the father ocean
Who survived last night?

A rose rise towards the immense blue,
perfuming the air and wind
with the mist of tears and despair.
A rose navigates to find a new horizon
in the blue breeze calm.
Her tears remind you of home—
that destroyed garden
on the shadows of the soldiers and bullets.

A rose kissed sea.
He went sailing into nothingness.
The moon welcomes you
with light, sunset, melodies.
The spirit creates the immensity of guitar strings.

# The Hidden Moon at Castlemaine

*For Janet Galbraith*

We will talk and write
through the Moon track, on any night;
our sister moon is made motionless by clouds.
She is locked up by rain and wind, on this winter day.
Janet and I, we left home for *Writing Through Fences.*
Here on this Aboriginal blue sky and red land,
espejo* of our own dream and passion.

Over there the stars are signal, hand and eyes,
lamp of our heart, speaking the rhythm
of who we are,
in this time of cruelty against of Nauru and Manus Island refugees...
We will talk and write
through the Moon track, on any night;
rise up our voices of solidarity,
lightly, with candles of sorrow, their bars of tears
and our verses will be read, through
the hidden Moon at Castlemaine.


We will talk and write
as a messenger of verses and passion,
through the Moon track, on any night;
for freedom and justice for the refugees in Detention Centres.

* espejo: mirror

# The Hidden Sky at Nauru at the Afternoon

To your words the Moon responds
within its own language.
Darkness in the afternoon at 5 o'clock.
I see Federico Garcia Lorca's verses
galloping through the sky at Castlemaine,
calling us poets to a Moon conference,
where action will be a track into our own blank papers.
Hope will grow in their eyes of the detainees.
Hope will embrace hearts in the sky at Nauru,
even if that hope is dying, in the hearts of detainees, men and
women in prison,
even when hope is dying in the eyes of the children at Nauru.
Hope will be a silent track; at dark the moon will embrace it.
And tears are a mirror of despair.
Games are needed when laughter is no longer in the human
soul.
What have we done to a child's heart to impose an evil code as
a name?
Pronouncing that evil code with a voice of power…boat
number.
The nurse said: ABJ123; Come here please!
Such a beautiful name is forbidden to be pronounced.
Such a beautiful name has to be hidden in this cruel system.
A beautiful name has to be hidden within
a list of consonants, vowels and numbers of brutal power.
A beautiful name is not a child, but only an evil-code for a
prison list.
Shame-Shame on you        PM
Shame-Shame on you        Australia.

# Bolivian Diary Ernesto Che Guevara

*A necessary Introduction by Samuel Lafferte*
*La selva boliviana tuvo los sueños heridos*
*Por décadas en siglos de exterminio y opresión.*
*Evo, es semilla, o piedra o patria libre*
*testamento del Che es un fusil*

"The only difference I would have with Che
is that he searched for
equality, justice with a gun in his hand".

Part 1...
9 & 10 September 1967
The day before was quiet, you said
but today, I think is a Guernica day,
for the animals and the river who embraced the waves
in a battle swimming for survival.
Weapons surrendered at the other side of the bank,
like soldiers of the unknown revolution.
An attack took place when Che and a mule crossed the
tangled streams and river rocks, camouflaged.
I lost my shoes during the crossing. Now I am in sandals.
Guernica mule drowned with rush of water.
Guernica airplanes and helicopters have flown over the area.
Guernica ambushes us with General Barrientos's Army.
Death comes as a bloody ambush shooting.
Death will fall there between water and mountains
as a seed of freedom,
or just as a jungle of corn hungry for what will be tomorrow.

# An ode to misery on this last night

*"We live in an age which is so possessed by demons that soon we shall only be able to do goodness and justice in the deepest secrecy, as if it were a crime"* —Franz Kafka.

The soul is a lake that goes dry in the middle of winter,
inhabited by so much melancholy, on the last night.
On the screen, the window of unhappiness.
I see Julian Assange transferred to the prison hospital.
The truth comes to us from prison, in the dying moments,
as from Bobby Sands, on the last day of his Hunger Strike,
covered only with a blanket.
As from Victor Jara, in the National Stadium, Chile,
his body riddled and hands broken by rifle butts.
Julian Assange, sentenced to death by the lies of power,
riddled with the apathy of our conscience.
Augusto Pinochet, released by the House of Lords
by agreement of Tony Blair and Jack Straw in March 2000.
Those on the other screen have not yet read Franz Kafka.

# The Sea in September

*Para Lionel Fogarty and Ali Cobby Eckermann*

The waves come softy, tender to my aching feet on the pathway.
The verses rise like the tide and go down again.
I embark on a verse from Canto Jondo.
The mountains look / a distant point.
I do not know if I'm a mountain, or that far point of absence.
Swim to the shore, almost without air,
overcome, and lying as in a verse from F. Holderin.
Waiting for my own death.
I asked among the ancients, the Heroes and Gods,
Why were you not there?
and now my soul is full of sadness...
My body is there, covered by sand and salt water.
I hear from the other side: Cesar Vallejo:
who shouts at me in his black voice, with his dark syllables,
with the day made night, it repeats like echoes of waves, coming to
my skin,
more here, more here. You are on the edge
and the ship can drag you to the sea.
These voices, these verses, these poets of mine and the world,
I give reason for a dream, to write it in the human heart.
I read and I cry these verses, until I stop, until I feel
the birth of verse, and weeping over these lines for my brother
Lionel Fogarty.
To feel that we still have reason to dream of living.
We had a dream now, where is the time for that dream?
September is a month of Allende's fire and memory.
Dreams, burned in the streets and courtyards, by soldiers.

Only the ashes rise up, smoke flying into the sky
like volantines entangled in the threads of pain.
I still think of that volantín (kite) that soars between flames and
the fear of life,
that September 11, 1973. As a witness to the tragedy we had to
live.

# 3

# Mother Earth Poems

Everything is blooming most recklessly; if it were voices instead
of colors, there would be an unbelievable shrieking into the heart
of the night.
—Rainer Maria Rilke

# The petals of the Cosmos

It's a galaxy
in the garden sink
the bees confused
they don't know if they swim or argue
about the pollen to drink
I leave that dangerous conversation

*2019*
*(Fragment of a day in the Garden).*

# Afternoons in January 2020, Australia

They have the smell of smoke from fires and desolation.
Wings with beheaded birds get tangled in Dantesque winds.
Koalas walk on burning ashes, fire burns their leaf food.
Orphans or refugees remain in their habitat.
Kangaroos flee the wind that burns the fields, the water.
While there is still debate about climate change,
here in the Library, the refugees by the fire
read, play and get distracted.
Not to mention words like Manus or Nauru
that still burn in our hearts.

*Adelaide January 2020*

# This New Year 2020 I wish all my friends, poets and activists to save humanity.

*In solidarity*

'Water is drops of life,
eyes of a koala without forest. Neither home,
humanity chooses to surrender to the clutches of the abyss.
We will be orphans of love, air, food,
and from the eyes in the waters of the dry river.'

*2019*

# The fire takes the forests (hills and Blue Mountains)

*As a current report by the Australia Media.*

But outside our window, fire burns koalas' dreams.
But outside our window, fire leaves kangaroos without paths to escape.
But outside our window, from the hot winds, daggers of destruction.
But outside our window, to the east, the fire made the flames as a hell.
It devours houses and villages.
 We are fallen leaves of the tree, devoured by the fire of evil

# I am a survivor harvesting verses in a vegetables garden

1
I find invisible waves and vastness of ink, on the blind page of
humanity.
We reached a shore where our footprints could no longer return.
Memory shrivelled like a dried fig in our dreams,
in the afternoon, our thoughts return to the cage of who we were.
Outside the window we become like birds,
lapping from the gutters of our old house,
then flying away to the branches of the past.
With wings on top of the roof, we wait for the horizon to fall,
on a flight towards what we were one day.

2
Resilience is beating in my soul.
I remember the handmade soup in our Abuela's kitchen,
created from the warmth of verses I shared with her at the table.
Her words were like pieces of capsicum, potatoes, garlic, a bit of
salt
falling into the scalding pot of life and tears,
listening to the voicelessness of our own souls, waiting so long in
that room.

3
We have been naked,
we only warm ourselves with the shadows of what we believe.
The war did not leave us any roads that led back home,
only deep ditches where we sheltered our loved ones
and from that time on, without knowing day from night,
we grasped the belief that humanity will save our dreams.

# The Bee in the cafe window

What are you doing there? I dare to ask.
Excuse me! I hit her on a wing
with the saliva of a consonant.
Fly back to the glass,
as if she was going to jump in emptiness.
half lying, try again,
falls off.
It falls and falls again.
Jump again fluttering,
to jump into the abyss of reality or in a verse.
I am sitting waiting for breakfast.
I no longer know what is most important:
eat or watch the performance.

She walks, flutters, like climbing the mountain of Everest.
Necessary preparation for the last performance.
Shake her legs and wings again.
Zigzag.
As if she finally finished her rehearsal.
But falls again,
tired of everything.
Body and soul shake.
Do bees have a heart?
Or is it the aroma of pollen?
What makes them throb with love and work?

In the middle of the final act,
it clings to the glass like an air acrobat.
Move along your destiny,
I think, watch her taste the petals
of clarity through glass.
Reality casts human shadows.
A motorcycle passes. She stays in her balance.

Again, she shakes her paws with the beauty of a lady.
Now her wings and legs applaud life.
I see its wings dust the air
in a pen that gives ink drops to my verse,

then, fall, shudder,
almost in the last greeting to her audience;
that is to say: to my verse and me.

At the foyer, voices create conversations.
The noise you cut makes them blind to the beauty of art.
I leave the table. I thank her.
When turning against the window
I see her fall to the stage of nothingness.
It shakes like an unannounced storm.
Exactly how my grandmother gave me her last look.

# The rain converses with the river

The rain converses with the river
in a dialogue falling to the sound of leaves, branches and wind.
I just went with my body, taking steps.
It was they who pronounced the poem,
while the footprints
from that shadow that I carry in me,
that bird bunging in my silence,
full of tears or rain, the leaves of the path.


II
I feel that I am today pieces of bark.
Shots on the road.
I see what there is and beyond.
As if the distance were
light trapped by clouds, pregnant with rain,
that reaches me between branches and leaves swinging,
in this cold sunset, with your hands clenched to the ropes of the
wind.
If I'm here, making a stop on the way,
I am an inhabitant of the look
that gives me a fresh throbbing of those that I feel,
at the edge of the river, sees the light fall, and the birds peck at the
green and wet grass
as if they've fed on the sunset reflection.
The clouds beat and catch the light. The rain rules over the back of
the sunset.
I embrace the wings of the birds and I shelter the inhabited wet
soul.

*29 May 2019*

# The Bulldozer and the Poet John Kinsella
at Christmas

*seasonal good stuff your way, j. hope 2017 works well for you and those things
improve for the entire planet! best, jk and tracy and tim*

I received an email on Christmas Day
from John and Tracy.
Wetlands attacke

d by bulldozers
which destroy the sacred sound
of the earth
and destroy the sacred spirit
of the ancestors laying down there—
pathway of roots, wind-roots and water-roots,
embracing our lives.
The poet reads his poem before the destruction of bushland on
Northlake Rd,
the noise behind him an attack against nature.
The verses read by the poet,
a protest to save our wetlands,
like a star in the wounded sky,
a voice of the dead trees, behind the poet, reading.
The bulldozer stopped like a final line of its poem,
an echo of words,
poem actions,
people actions,
poet-actions against the bulldozer of power and greed.

# Crying at the sea shore

I want to cry as you sweat on the injured skin.

I want to cry with the eyes of children

who have lost everything in the war.

I want to weep between bombs and the death of the dead

that no one will bury.

In any holder of the market of international communications,

I want to weep, in the water mixed with the blood of that invisible
puddle of pain.

With the clothes that I have put on, as a survivor of the invasion that
destroyed my home.

I want to cry with the tears of the fallen,

with the cry of the destruction of my cities, countries and the soul of
my neighborhood.

I want to mourn what I lost in my today, and perhaps the morning
time is gone.

Bread and water,

the farewell, what was not said and hidden from me.

I want to cry for my protest,

because of my voice that is voiceless,

through the empty streets, outbreaks of peace.

By the calm sea and the wind, that is only breeze from my tears
this afternoon.

I want to cry because I'm sitting here like a pilgrim of everyday
life,

in front of the sea writing a poem about crying.

I want to cry for my little broken things like my watch, my pants,

the chain of my bicycle, my teapot that goes like a wild train,
screaming that dies in the

waiting of all that did not reach to travel.

I want to cry for all my grandchildren who die in these invading
wars,

of this post-colonial time.

I want to cry, even if you look at me, I'm crying, for photos of
children from Aleppo.

On this page, that wet my verse in this instant of a sunny April
afternoon,

I am crying, from the road, through the empty streets,

between debris of the speech of the invading power.

I want to cry because of the calm sea and the wind, that is only
breeze from my tears.

I want to cry because I'm sitting here like a pilgrim of everyday life. In front of the sea writing a poem about crying.

I want to cry for my little triviality of my broken things like my watch, my pants,

the chain of my bicycle,

my boiling teapot, like

the wild cry of a train that dies, in the waiting for all that did not reach the trip.

I want to cry for all my grandchildren who die in these invading wars

of this post-colonial time.

I am crying from the road.

I'm crying dry tears with the wind that saw me cry.

I want to cry all the pain in Syria, Yemen, Afghanistan and Venezuela.

I want to mourn all the injustices of Nauru refugee camp.

I want to mourn for the invasions of ancestral lands.

I want to cry, to come back to live, to suffer and to love.

For what they have destroyed in me, snatched, lied and deceived,

I want to cry with my dry tears,

the dryness radiating from my mother's dead soul, already late my mother Earth.

I want to cry in this seat, facing the sea where I left the sunset of April.

## ...And my hands are all that I have...by Victor Jara

I have come to the garden. My hands are all that I have,
my sweat and my bread, as a verse of Victor Jara.
The fruit loosened leaves,
orphaned, become fertilizer wings.
its inbound roots breathe the confusion of life,
talk with cabbage and ask
if I can write a poem in their leaves, left there.
The sun winks at me and drops my pencil out of nowhere.
I write it as a mystery gift of life
that gives everything in a moment.

# The sun is an orange hanging from a branch in my garden

The sun is an orange hanging from a branch in my garden.
Heavy rain leaves invisible nests.
As wet birds, over green leaves,
fall hungry to the wet ground to peck
and the worms, drunken in those dreams
from moisture, begin to fly.


The sun is an orange hanging from a branch in my garden
My frozen hand takes it
as a fruit, that planet starts rolling down
as a sweet fire,
savoring the air and the simple life
of being a sun, hanging in my garden.

# I'm a citizen of the earth

I'm not an ethnic.......I was born on the Mapudungun land in 1957.

I' m not a refugee.....my suitcases were full of memory, love, families' tears and a lost kiss.

I'm a political prisoner from Pinochet's regime....my cell was a dark and painful space filled with those days of freedom.

I no longer have the permanent visa to enter Australia.

I'm only an F... citizen.

I'm a citizen on this battered land,

walking with broken verses to pronounce to you,

howling the hope that still grows like a scorched seed,

in the forest burned by the silence of the water,

arriving to the shore long ago.

# Before the rivers spoke with the trees

I would tell you if someone crossed

to take water or memory. Leaves fall.

 Before silence abounded in my land,
 nobody needed to talk.

The words were birds going out to swim

in a cloud, and at dusk they returned to the river.

Rather, they fell to the heart of the fish

who abounded on its banks.

And the poets went and took the words, like live fish,

to share them at the sunset table—

and read the stories and poems of the day

before the earth was a mother.

Today she is a widow of the past.

And we are orphaned by poems and stories

which our ancestors sang to us without paper.

Through the trees they were sacred giants.

Mountains in our dreams.

Somebody stole the river.

## 'So, for me, freedom and the sea / They will respond to the dark heart' by Pablo Neruda

I try to write about what is planted in the heart of the garden.
My destiny will be a cocoon to love.
The tears, water that is the daily irrigation of what I love.
The wind is my footsteps, that stop meowing, the smells of the shade.
Fall in the rose garden.

I am a missing word,
a name pulverized by numbers of statistics,
a bleeding heart on the barbed wire,
a wave that roars death in its swing,
survivor on the brink of cruelty.

I have a citizenship that opens the wounds of yesterday.
I have a citizenship that imprisons those who seek asylum.
I have a citizenship that imprisons the ancestral spirit.
I have a citizenship that darkens the heart
and leaves us speechless.
Crying is the only protest that keeps us alive.

# Eight feathers of a dead bird

Eight feathers of a dead bird.
Eight feathers without flight or eternity.
Orphaned fallen bird,
to the juicy bite of the garden.
Eight feathers of the air,
  They land in the death of taste
of that orange, food in the eyes
of the bird devoured by circumstances.

Fall like we're sad dawn
sinking inland,
root of happy wings that went in flight.

# kookaburra 's song

We dialogues of dry rivers and trees of crying.
The word is the appraisal of surplus value.
A verse is sinking into the laws of the hypocrisy boat.
We are no longer citizens or poets; but consumers
in a supermarket
on Earth.

# Notes

'This afternoon I'm a character in Fyodor Dostoyevsky': translated by Tamryn Bennett

'What to do when you lose faith': I wrote this poem for Sr Janet Mead, a dear friend who welcomed us into her Romero community as a political refugee's family from Chile. She died on 26 January 2022.

'I am the Size of What I see': this poem is a Tribute to Ernesto Cardenal, a Nicaraguan Priest, Poet and a Former Minister of Culture of the Nicaragua Sandinista, 1983.

Also my gratitude to Gloria Gabuardi and Fracisco de Asis Fernandez, organisers of the International Granada Poetry Festival, Nicaragua, and to the Australia Arts Council for the grants to travel to Nicaragua, Mexico and Cuba.

# Acknowledgments

Poems from this collection have appeared in the following publications: *Cordite, Eureka Street, The Saturday Paper, Best of Australian Poems 2021, Verity La, Social Aternatives, Australian Poetry Anthology, Puentes Review, Canto Planetario, Erza-Poetry Magazine.*

www.ingramcontent.com/pod-product-compliance
Lightning Source LLC
Chambersburg PA
CBHW030940090426
42737CB00007B/485